Encounters with God

The First and Second
Epistles of Paul
the Apostle to TIMOTHY
and TITUS

Encounters with God Study Guide Series

The Gospel of Matthew

The Gospel of Mark

The Gospel of Luke

The Gospel of John

The Book of Acts

The Book of Romans

The First Epistle of Paul the Apostle to the Corinthians

The Second Epistle of Paul the Apostle to the Corinthians

The Epistle of Paul the Apostle to the Galatians

The Epistle of Paul the Apostle to the Ephesians

The Epistle of Paul the Apostle to the Philippians

The Epistles of Paul the Apostle to the Colossians and Philemon

The First and Second Epistles of Paul the Apostle to the Thessalonians

The First and Second Epistles of Paul the Apostle to Timothy and Titus

The Epistle of Paul the Apostle to the Hebrews

The Epistle of James

The First and Second Epistles of Peter

The First, Second, and Third Epistles of John and Jude

The Revelation of Jesus Christ

Encounters with God

The First and Second Epistles of Paul the Apostle to TIMOTHY and TITUS

Published in Nashville, Tennessee, by Thomas Nelson. Thomas Nelson is a registered
trademark of Thomas Nelson, Inc.

Thomas Nelson, Inc. titles may be purchased in bulk for educational, business,
fund-raising, or sales promotional use. For information, please e-mail
SpecialMarkets@ThomasNelson.com.

ISBN 978-1-4185-2651-1

Printed in the United States of America

HB 08.17.2023

CONTENTS

AN INTRODUCTION TO THE FIRST AND SECOND EPISTLES TO TIMOTHY AND THE EPISTLE TO TITUS

This study guide covers three epistles from the apostle Paul to close colleagues in the ministry: Timothy and Titus. Each epistle is a fairly short and personal letter. These very likely are the last letters written by Paul. Taken together, they are called the Pastoral Epistles.

Both Timothy and Titus had traveled in evangelistic ministry with the apostle Paul. They each had been sent by Paul to pastor specific churches. Paul wrote to them near the end of his life to encourage them personally, to warn them against the teachings of heretics who seem to be infusing pagan speculations and Jewish legalism into the gospel message, and to impress upon them the need for establishing structure and discipline in the churches they were leading. The three letters likely were written in this order: 1 Timothy, Titus, 2 Timothy.

Although the letters were written to individuals, they were intended to be read aloud to the churches where Timothy and Titus were ministering. Timothy was ministering in Ephesus, and Titus was on the island of Crete.

Timothy. Timothy was a native of Lystra, a city in Asia Minor. His father was a Gentile, but his mother and grandmother were Jewish. He was taught Scripture from an early age (Acts 16:1; 2 Tim. 1:5, 3:15). Paul was Timothy's primary mentor and very possibly the one who led Timothy to personal faith in Jesus Christ, since Paul refers to Timothy as his spiritual child (1 Cor. 4:17; 2 Tim. 2:1).

Timothy traveled extensively with Paul and at times served as the apostle's representative to the churches at Corinth, Philippi, and Thessalonica—and perhaps others (1 Cor. 4:17, 16:10; Phil. 2:19–24; 1 Thess. 3:2,6). In Ephesus Timothy was not the long-term senior pastor, but he did have significant pastoral influence over the church there, and he appears to have been given great authority in areas related to doctrinal and organizational stability. Paul had taught for at least two years in Ephesus, and Timothy appears to have been given the authority to speak in Paul's name and to give the loving, firm direction Paul himself would have given if he was present.

Both letters to Timothy were intended to counter false teachers who were troubling the church at Ephesus. Paul refuted heretical doctrines and practices and made strong statements about the importance of guarding against further heresy, living in a godly manner, and clarifying proper church practices. In the second letter Paul wrote to strengthen Timothy's loyalty to the Lord Jesus Christ and to ask Timothy to join him in Rome.

Titus. Titus was a Greek convert and one of Paul's first Gentile co-laborers. He played a significant role in the development of the early church. Titus was an uncircumcised Gentile who accompanied Paul to Jerusalem. There, he provided witness to the Jewish believers that Gentiles could also experience salvation by grace alone, apart from circumcision. When a difficult situation arose in the church in Corinth, Paul sent Titus there to handle the situation and his accomplishments in Corinth were of great encouragement to Paul (1 Cor. 1:11, 5:1; 2 Cor. 7:6,13; 8:6,16, 23; 12:18). Titus apparently was a resourceful leader with good organizational skills.

At the time he wrote to Titus, Paul had entrusted Titus to organize and instruct the new converts in the church that had been established on the Mediterranean island of Crete. The moral decadence in Crete was well-known throughout the region, and Paul knew that Titus would face significant opposition in his ministry there. His letter gives Titus authorization and guidance regarding the doctrine, government, and godly behavior Paul desired to see among the believers.

All three of the letters to Timothy and Titus weave together theology and practical instruction. Paul was intent on right doctrine being applied rightly to produce right living.

About the Author, the Apostle Paul. Paul identified himself as the author of each letter (1 Tim. 1:1; 2 Tim. 1:1; Titus 1:1). Some have questioned Paul's authorship since these letters have a wider vocabulary and range of style than some of the other letters ascribed to Paul. It should be noted, however, that Paul had a very high level of education and wide exposure to various groups in the Mediterranean world. He may also have dictated these letters to a secretary (or amanuensis), who may have been given some freedom in the precise wording of the letters. Most importantly, the letters are consistent with Paul's general message to the churches.

The letters are thought to have been written between AD 62 and 67. Although the Book of Acts does not detail what happened during the last years of Paul's life, historians have generally concluded that Paul was first imprisoned in Rome about AD 60-63. Then he was set free for a period. Both 1 Timothy and Titus present Paul as traveling freely in the eastern Mediterranean region—to Ephesus (1 Tim. 1:3, 3:14), Crete (Titus 1:5), and

Nicopolis in the eastern Adriatic Sea (Titus 3:12). The letters we know as 1 Timothy and Titus were written during this period of freedom, probably between AD 63 and AD 64. Paul appears to have been imprisoned again in 65–67 AD. He wrote 2 Timothy during this imprisonment. Early church tradition states that the Roman emperor Nero executed Paul in late 67 or early 68.

When taken as a whole, Paul's letters addressed both the triumphs and difficulties encountered by the first-century Christians, many of whom faced intense persecution for their faith. The issues Paul addressed in his letters to the first-century church are no less important to today's believers. Paul laid a very practical foundation for *how* to live the Christian life in the face of struggles, temptations, and heresies. His personal decision to know and obey Christ Jesus no matter the cost remains an example to all who call themselves Christians. "I in Christ and Christ in me" was Paul's unwavering theme song.

An Overview of Our Study of the First and Second Epistles to Timothy and The Epistle to Titus

This study guide presents seven lessons drawn from the New Testament books of 1 and 2 Timothy and Titus. It elaborates upon the commentary included in the *Blackaby Study Bible*:

Lesson #1: The Importance of Sound Doctrine

Lesson #2: Praying for Those in Authority

Lesson #3: Qualifications for Church Leadership

Lesson #4: Women in the Early Church

Lesson #5: Marks of a Truly Rich Life

Lesson #6: The Pursuit of Righteousness

Lesson #7: The Mercy of God

Personal or Group Use. These lessons are offered for personal study and reflection or for small-group Bible study. The study questions asked may be answered by an individual reader or used as a foundation for group discussion. A segment titled "Notes to Leaders of Small Groups" is included at the back of this book to help those leading a group study of this material.

Before you embark on this study, we encourage you to read in full the statement in the *Blackaby Study Bible* titled "How to Study the Bible." Our contention is always that the Bible is unique among all literature. It is God's definitive word for humanity. The Bible is:

* *inspired*—"God-breathed"

* *authoritative*—absolutely the final word on any spiritual matter

- *the plumb line of truth*—the standard against which all human activity and reasoning must be evaluated

The Bible is fascinating in that it has remarkable diversity but also remarkable unity. Its books were penned by a diverse assortment of authors representing a variety of languages and cultures, and it contains a number of literary forms. But the Bible's message from cover to cover is clear, consistent, and unified.

More than mere words on a page, the Bible is an encounter with God Himself. No book is more critical to your life. The very essence of the Bible is the Lord Himself.

The Holy Spirit speaks through the Bible. He also communicates during your time of prayer, in your life circumstances, and through the church. Read your Bible in an attitude of prayer, and allow the Holy Spirit to make you aware of God's activity in and through your personal life. Write down what you learn, meditate on it, and adjust your thoughts, attitudes, and behavior accordingly. Look for ways every day to apply the truth of God's Word to your circumstances and relationships. God is not random; He is orderly and intentional in the way He speaks to you.

Be encouraged—the Bible is *not* too difficult for the average person to understand if that person asks the Holy Spirit for help. (Furthermore, not even the most brilliant person can fully understand the Bible apart from the Holy Spirit's help!) God desires for you to know Him and to know His Word. Every person who reads the Bible can learn from it. The person who will receive *maximum* benefits from reading and studying the Bible, however, is the person who:

- *is born again* (John 3:3,5). Those who are born again and have received the gift of His Spirit have a distinct advantage in understanding the deeper truths of God's Word.

- *has a heart that desires to learn God's truth.* Your attitude greatly influences the outcome of Bible study. Resist the temptation to focus on what others have said about the Bible. Allow the Holy Spirit to guide you as you study God's Word for yourself.

- *has a heart that seeks to obey God.* The Holy Spirit teaches the most to those who desire to apply what they learn.

Begin your Bible study with prayer, asking the Holy Spirit to guide your thoughts and to impress upon you what is on God's heart. Then make plans to adjust your life immediately to obey the Lord fully.

As you read and study the Bible, your purpose is not to *create* meaning, but to *discover* the meaning of the text with the Holy Spirit's guidance. Ask yourself, "What did the author have in mind? How was this applied by those who first heard these words?" Especially in your study of Paul's letters, look for ways in which the truths can be applied directly to your personal, practical, daily Christian walk and to the life of your church.

At times you may find it helpful to consult other passages of the Bible (made available in the center columns in the *Blackaby Study Bible*), or the commentary that is in the margins of the *Blackaby Study Bible*.

Keep in mind always that Bible study is not primarily an exercise for acquiring information but an opportunity for transformation. Bible study is your opportunity to encounter God and to be changed in His presence. When God speaks to your heart, nothing remains the same. Jesus said, "He who has ears to hear, let him hear" (Matt. 13:9). Choose to have ears that desire to hear!

The B-A-S-I-Cs of Each Study in This Guide. Each lesson in this study guide has five segments, using the word BASIC as an acronym. The word BASIC does not allude to elementary or simple, but rather to foundational. These studies extend the concepts that are part of the *Blackaby Study Bible* commentary and are focused on key aspects of what it means to be a Christ-follower in today's world. The BASIC acronym stands for:

B = *Bible Focus.* This segment presents the central passage for the lesson and a general explanation that covers the central theme or concern.

A = *Application for Today.* This segment has a story or illustration related to current-day events with questions that link the Bible text to today's issues, problems, and concerns.

S = *Supplementary Scriptures to Consider.* In this segment other Bible verses related to the general theme of the lesson are explored.

I = *Introspection and Implications.* In this segment questions are asked that lead to deeper reflection about one's personal faith journey and life experiences.

C = *Communicating the Good News.* In this segment challenging questions point to ways the lesson's truth might be lived out and shared with others, whether to win the lost or build up the church.

LESSON #1

THE IMPORTANCE OF SOUND DOCTRINE

Doctrine: a rule or principle that forms the basis of a belief system

B
Bible Focus

> *As I urged you when I went into Macedonia—remain in Ephesus that you may charge some that they teach no other doctrine, nor give heed to fables and endless genealogies, which cause disputes rather than godly edification which is in faith. Now the purpose of the commandment is love from a pure heart, from a good conscience, and from sincere faith, from which some, having strayed, have turned aside to idle talk, desiring to be teachers of the law, understanding neither what they say nor the things which they affirm.*
>
> *But we know that the law is good if one uses it lawfully, knowing this: that the law is not made for a righteous person, but for the lawless and insubordinate, for the ungodly and for sinners, for the unholy and profane, for murderers of fathers and murderers of mothers, for manslayers, for fornicators, for sodomites, for kidnappers, for liars, for perjurers, and if there is any other thing that is contrary to sound doctrine, according to the glorious gospel of the blessed God which was committed to my trust (1 Tim. 1:3–11).*

The apostle Paul had taught in Ephesus for two years, but at the time he wrote his first letter to Timothy, he was again traveling in ministry. Timothy, his long-time colleague and frequent representative, had been left behind in Ephesus to continue to give doctrinal and organizational stability to the church there. It appears that shortly after Paul left Ephesus, teachers arrived on the scene to offer a message that was a mixture of regulations from Judaism, speculations from pagan Gnosticism, and genuine Christian doctrine. These false teachers created discord, and hearing of it, Paul wrote not only to encourage Timothy but also to provide a document Timothy could read authoritatively to the church.

Paul wrote first and foremost that the purpose of God's commandments is to produce genuine godly love in the human heart. Idle speculations, fables, and a preoccupation with one's ancestry do not produce love but rather, disputes. In just a few sentences, Paul gave a template for evaluating every doctrine-oriented message a person might ever hear. We are wise to ask, "Does the message produce godly love, or does it generate discord?" The message that produces godly love is the right message!

Paul then brilliantly provided a succinct reason for the law of Moses: to bring about conviction in the hearts of those who are failing in their love for

God or other people. Paul listed ten categories of people that are corrected by the law. These ten categories of people line up with the Ten Commandments.

The law, Paul wrote, addresses those who are lawless, insubordinate, ungodly, unholy, and profane—in others words those who do not honor the Lord their God, who have other gods before Him, make for themselves carved images, who take the name of the Lord in vain, and who refuse to keep the Sabbath holy. The law confronts those who are the murderers of fathers and mothers, those who do not honor their fathers and mothers. The law stands against those who are manslayers, fornicators, sodomites, kidnappers (also translated thieves), liars, and perjurers—those who commit murder and adultery, covet and steal, and bear false witness against their neighbors.

Keeping the law is not the end game for the Christian, but rather the foundation for "the glorious gospel of the blessed God." Paul pointed toward a message of good news that creates love in the human heart. Whereas the law stands against sin, the gospel creates newness of spirit—it generates sincere faith and purity of heart. Whereas the law convicts, the gospel calls a person freely to receive and extend forgiveness, which produces a clean or "good" conscience. Paul pointed Timothy toward sound teaching that is based upon the law but not limited to it. The word for *sound* in this passage, *hugiainein,* literally means *health-giving.* The law stands against anything that tears apart the fabric of human life, and the gospel in turn, promotes everything that fosters healing and wholeness.

Both the law and the gospel were vital, Paul taught; one does not negate or replace the other. Even so, the two are different in purpose and effect. Whereas the law defines sin and the need for reconciliation, the gospel presents salvation for the sinner and offers the means of reconciliation. Whereas the law contains and restrains, the gospel unleashes the human spirit and allows it to soar. It is the gospel that has true transformative power to those who believe.

Many believers today experience a degree of tension between following both God's commandments and the traditions of the faith, and living in freedom in Christ Jesus. We each want to be free of anything that might shackle us or keep us from fulfilling our potential. However, we also know we need moorings and rules to keep us from dashing our futures against the rocks of error and from destroying relationships in our haste for personal accomplishment. The exact balance between what is fluid and what is fixed is often difficult to determine.

How much of the Old Testament law are we to keep as believers in Christ Jesus? Which laws apply to us and which don't?

How can we discern which teachings are diverting us from the true gospel message with the potential to destroy us individually and as a church?

How can we stay pure in our love, clear in our consciences, and sincere in our faith?

These questions are just as pertinent to us today as to believers in Paul's time.

A
Application for Today

"I just don't seem to have time for personal daily devotionals," a woman confessed to her spiritual mentor. "My life is so busy I seem to be racing from the time I get up to the time I go to bed."

"Do you truly *want* to spend time with the Lord?" her mentor asked sincerely.

"Oh, yes!" the woman said, secretly hoping that *wanting* to have a daily devotional time counted for something.

"Then keep a time log for this coming work week," her mentor said. "Write down everything you do on a time schedule that is blocked out in fifteen-minute segments. Write every hour. I know this will take some effort, but probably not more than a minute for each waking hour."

The woman agreed. She was certain that her schedule would amaze and overwhelm her mentor. However, the next Sunday evening when she met with her mentor she opened their conversation with these words, "OK, so I *do* have time for devotionals."

"Oh?" her mentor said.

The woman confessed, "I felt really guilty every time I wrote down things such as 'read e-mail jokes, surfed the 'net, watched a soap opera while eating lunch, watched TV for an hour in the evening, talked about trivial things with someone at the water cooler,' and 'read a chapter of a novel before going to bed.'"

"Were you surprised at your use of time?" her mentor asked.

"Very!" the woman said. "I've been spending at least three hours a day on things that are fun or interesting, but which have nothing to do with feeding my spirit for eternal benefit, and I didn't think I had a spare minute."

What about you?

The apostle Paul warned against heeding "fables and endless genealogies" and "idle talk." These things were being used as a filter for interpreting or giving added meaning to the Christian life. To what extent do you rely upon the common-sense wisdom of natural man, the principles taught by pop psychology gurus, or the conclusions of secular media talk show hosts for your worldview or for your interpretation of Scripture? How much time each

day do you spend taking in the Word of God or reading or hearing exposi-
tions of sound doctrine?

You may benefit from keeping your own time log for the coming work
week.

S
Supplementary Scriptures to Consider

As he had advised Timothy, the apostle Paul told Titus, too, to avoid
foolish disputes and contentions, calling them unprofitable and useless for
the gospel. Paul took a second step with Titus, however, telling him how to
"reject a divisive man":

> Avoid foolish disputes, genealogies, contentions, and strivings
> about the law; for they are unprofitable and useless. Reject a
> divisive man after the first and second admonition, knowing
> that such a person is warped and sinning, being self-con-
> demned (Titus 3:9–11).

• What is the difference between "contention" and a discussion based on
  differing viewpoints?

• How does Paul say a divisive person should be admonished?

• In what ways do people who are divisive condemn themselves?

• What perceived profit or benefit might be linked to disputes, genealogies, and contentions? Why do these perceived benefits turn out to be hollow and useless?

The apostle Paul wrote this to Timothy about persevering in right doctrine:

> Hold fast the pattern of sound words which you have heard from me, in faith and love which are in Christ Jesus. That good thing which was committed to you, keep by the Holy Spirit who dwells in us. (2 Tim. 1:13–14)

• How do we "keep by the Holy Spirit" the truth we have heard and believed?

• Who speaks into your life a "pattern of sound words"? How do you know with certainty these are words of truth?

The apostle Paul taught that Scripture is highly beneficial in several different ways:

> All Scripture is given by inspiration of God, and is profitable for doctrine, for reproof, for correction, for instruction in righteousness, that the man of God may be complete, thoroughly equipped for every good work. (2 Tim. 3:16)

• Recall an experience in which you were equipped for good work because you read and applied Scripture.

• Scripture tells us what to believe (doctrine), what is contrary to God's will (reproof), what needs to be changed for "natural man" to become "spiritual man" (correction), and how to live in right standing with God (instruction in righteousness). Cite at least one practical example of the way you have benefited from a study of Scripture in each of these four areas:

Doctrine:

Reproof:

Correction:

Instruction in Righteousness:

The apostle Paul warned about specific things that detour believers from genuine faith:

> Now the Spirit expressly says that in latter times some will depart from the faith, giving heed to deceiving spirits and doctrines of demons, speaking lies in hypocrisy, having their own conscience seared with a hot iron, forbidding to marry, and commanding to abstain from foods which God created to be received with thanksgiving by those who believe and know the truth. For every creature of God is good, and nothing is to be refused if it is received with thanksgiving; for it is sanctified by the word of God and prayer. (1 Tim. 4:1–5)

• How does a person refrain from "giving heed to deceiving spirits and doctrines of demons"?

• How does a person keep their conscience from being "seared with a hot iron"?

- Paul identified beliefs related to "forbidding to marry" and abstaining from certain foods as having potential to lead people away from the faith. In what ways do you perceive this might this happen?

The apostle Paul gave a profile of the person who does not heed a doctrine that produces godliness:

> If anyone teaches otherwise and does not consent to wholesome words, even the words of our Lord Jesus Christ, and to the doctrine which accords with godliness, he is proud, knowing nothing, but is obsessed with disputes and arguments over words, from which come envy, strife, reviling, evil suspicions, useless wranglings of men of corrupt minds an destitute of the truth, who suppose that godliness is a means of gain. From such withdraw yourself (1 Tim. 6:3–5).

- How might a believer withdraw in a godly manner from a proud, contentious person?

- Have you ever encountered a person who is obsessed with disputes and arguments? How does such a person impact a group? What did you do? What was the outcome—short-term and long-term?

I
Introspection and Implications

1. How do you distinguish between being Law-abiding (keeping the law of the Old Testament) and being legalistic?

2. How does the law of God impact your life personally and practically?

3. What do you consider to be sound doctrine?

C
Communicating the Good News

What is your doctrine on these issues related directly to evangelism:

• Who is Jesus?

• Why did Jesus die?

• What is required to be reconciled to God?

LESSON #2

PRAYING FOR THOSE
IN AUTHORITY

*Authority: one who has the
right or power to enforce
rules or give orders*

B
Bible Focus

> This charge I commit to you, son Timothy . . . that . . . you
> may wage the good warfare. . . .
> I exhort first of all that supplications, prayers, interces-
> sions, and giving of thanks be made for all men, for kings and
> all who are in authority, that we may lead a quiet and peace-
> able life in all godliness and reverence. For this is good and
> acceptable in the sight of God our Savior, who desires all men
> to be saved and to come to the knowledge of the truth. For
> there is one God and one Mediator between God and men, the
> Man Christ Jesus, who gave Himself a ransom for all, to be
> testified in due time, for which I was appointed a preacher and
> an apostle—I am speaking the truth in Christ and not lying—
> a teacher of the Gentiles in faith and truth (1 Tim. 1:18,
> 2:1–7).

This very brief passage from Paul's first letter to Timothy is like a cascad-
ing waterfall—one truth spilling over to a related truth, in turn spilling over
to yet another truth.

Paul charged Timothy to wage the good warfare, or in other words, to
fight the good fight or engage in the winning military campaign. The fight is
for the gospel and all of its life-giving, wholeness-producing, spiritually-
enriching power. The fight is simultaneously *against* the devil and all the
forces of evil that might thwart the gospel. To win this war is to be successful in ministry.

How is the good fight fought? In prayer. Paul exhorts Timothy and the
church he leads to pray, and specifically to engage in supplications (identify-
ing their needs and framing them into requests), prayer (going to God with
their requests), and intercession (petitioning God in intimate conversation),
all with an attitude of thanksgiving.

For whom are we to pray? For all people we encounter and for those in
authority over us.

Why do we pray for these? Because they hold the key to our being able to
live a quiet and peaceful life. Our ability to lead calm, purposeful lives is
directly related to our ability to live favorably with those we routinely
encounter as neighbors, employers, co-workers, clients, vendors, customers,
and colleagues. Our ability to lead godly lives is also directly related to those
in authority over us. Those who make and enforce the laws that frame our
society determine to a great extent the degree to which we can freely exercise our faith.

Why desire a peaceful, quiet life of godly behavior and reverence? Because this is our greatest witness to the world! It is the overall witness of our lives as Christians that attracts sinners to Christ, far more so than our occasional words of testimony. The world watches how Christians *live* and when the world sees Christians loving one another in peace and harmony, the world is drawn toward that way of life. The attractiveness of our life in Christ gives us a platform for introducing others to Christ Jesus so they might receive Him as their Savior.

We must remain acutely aware, Paul taught, that God honors godliness and reverence, and that God desires for all men to be saved. This does not mean that all men are automatically saved or that all will respond favorably to the gospel. It does mean that we at all times must have the heart of God—we must *desire* to live in a way that attracts lost souls to Christ Jesus.

What is the heart of the message we are to share with the world? That there is only one God and that there is only one mediator between God and men. Who is that one mediator? Christ Jesus. How is He the mediator? He gave His life as a ransom.

What is our responsibility? To testify to this truth with faith—we are to herald or proclaim this truth at every opportune moment given to us.

In a nutshell, Paul gave Timothy the outline for successful ministry: pray, live a godly life, and proclaim the supremacy and uniqueness of Christ Jesus our Savior. The successful ministry belongs not only to ordained clergy, but to every lay person who calls himself or herself Christian.

Are you engaged in good warfare today?

For whom are you praying and how are you praying for them?

How are you living?

To whom are you witnessing?

A
Application for Today

One of the greatest prayers offered for secular leaders in the history of the church is the prayer written by Clement of Rome in his first letter to the church at Corinth. The prayer was written about AD 90 as a prayer to be offered for the Emperor of the Roman empire. It was written at a time when the savagery of Emperor Domitian was still very fresh in the peoples' minds:

Prayer for the Emperor

"You, Lord and Master, have given our rulers and governors
the power of sovereignty through Your excellent and unspeak-
able might, that we, knowing the glory and honor which You

have given them, may submit ourselves unto them, in nothing resisting Your will. Grant unto them, therefore, O Lord, health, peace, concord, stability, that they may administer the government which You have given them, without failure. For You, O heavenly Master, King of the Ages, give to the sons of men glory and honor and power over all things that are upon the earth. Lord, direct their counsel according to that which is good and well-pleasing in Your sight, that, administering the power which You have given them in peace and gentleness with godliness, they may obtain Your favor. You, alone are able to do these things, and things far more exceeding good than these for us! Therefore we praise You through the High Priest and Guardian of our souls, Jesus Christ, through whom be the glory and the majesty unto You both now and for all generations, and for ever and ever. Amen."

What a generous and loving prayer this is! Note how closely it mirrors the apostle Paul's words to Timothy and the church at Ephesus.

How are you praying for the leaders of *your* nation—both those with whom you agree and those with whom you disagree, those for who you voted, and those for whom you did not vote?

Write out a prayer for those who are in authority over you.

S
Supplementary Scriptures to Consider

The apostle Paul wrote this to Titus:

Remind them to be subject to rulers and authorities, to obey, to be ready for every good work, to speak evil of no one, to be peaceable, gentle, showing all humility to all men. For we ourselves were also once foolish, disobedient, deceived, serving various lusts and pleasures, living in malice and envy, hateful and hating one another. But when the kindness and the love of God our Savior toward man appeared, not by works of righteousness which we have done, but according to His mercy He saved us, through the washing of regeneration and renewing of the Holy Spirit, whom He poured out on us abundantly through Jesus Christ our Savior, that having been justified by His grace we should become heirs according to the hope of eternal life (Titus 3:1–7).

• Give a practical example of the way in which you seek to do each of these things:

Be subject to rulers and authorities:

Obey:

Be ready for every good work:

Speak evil of no one:

Be peaceable and gentle, showing all humility:

• What do the phrases below mean to you?

Washing of Regeneration:

Renewing of the Holy Spirit:

To a slave living at the time of Paul, the immediate person in authority was the slave's master. Paul wrote this to Titus:

> Exhort bondservants to be obedient to their own masters, to be
> well pleasing in all things, not answering back, not pilfering,
> but showing all good fidelity, that they may adorn the doctrine
> of God our Savior in all things (Titus 2:9–10).

• How might your good works influence those in authority over *you*? What is the difference between doing good works as unto the Lord and doing good works as a means of pandering or soliciting favor?

• How might a slave influence a master to accept Christ? Do these same deeds apply to modern-day employees and employers?

The apostle Paul was quick to note that one of the most important forms of witness is good works:

> This is a faithful saying, and these things I want you to affirm constantly, that those who have believed in God should be careful to maintain good works. These things are good and profitable to men (Titus 3:8).

• What is to be gained by displaying our belief in God through good works?

• What helps you *maintain* good works over time and through difficult times?

On the matter of praying, Paul added this in his letter to Timothy:

> I desire therefore that the men pray everywhere, lifting up holy hands, without wrath and doubting (1 Tim. 2:8).

• Jewish men prayed with their hands lifted at ninety degrees from the elbows, open palms facing outward. This was a sign that the person held no weapons and was holding nothing back from God. It was a prayer position of transparent surrender. What does it mean to you in your payer life to "lift up holy hands" to God as you pray?

I
Introspection and Implications

1. Identify three people who have some type of authority over you.

   1.

2.

3.

Next to each name or title of the person above, identify two things you believe you should pray for that person.

2. In what ways do you find it difficult to pray for elected officials with whom you disagree politically?

3. What do you perceive to be the balance between voicing or demonstrating your disagreement with a political position and praying for those in political authority?

C
Communicating the Good News

In what ways might all opportunities to offer prayer in public be opportunities to present the gospel?

Why is it important for lost souls to hear righteous people pray? What are the most effective prayers for a sinner to hear from the mouth of a Christian?

LESSON #3

QUALIFICATIONS FOR CHURCH LEADERSHIP

Reverent: feeling or expressing profound respect or awe

B
Bible Focus

*This is a faithful saying: If a man desires the position of a
bishop, he desires a good work. A bishop then must be blameless, the husband of one wife, temperate, sober-minded, of
good behavior, hospitable, able to teach; not given to wine,
not violent, not greedy for money, but gentle, not quarrelsome,
not covetous; one who rules his own house well, having his
children in submission with all reverence (for if a man does
not know how to rule his own house, how will he take care of
the church of God?); not a novice, lest being puffed up with
pride he fall into the same condemnation as the devil. More-
over he must have a good testimony among those who are
outside, lest he fall into reproach and the snare of the devil.*

*Likewise deacons must be reverent, not double-tongued, not
given to much wine, not greedy for money, holding the mystery
of the faith with a pure conscience. But let these also first be
tested; then let them serve as deacons, being found blameless.
Likewise, their wives must be reverent, not slanderers, temperate, faithful in all things. Let deacons be the husbands of one
wife, ruling their children and their own houses well. For
those who have served well as deacons obtain for themselves
a good standing and great boldness in the faith which is in
Christ Jesus (1 Tim. 3:1–13).*

Not every person is called to lead, and not all those who are natural
leaders in the world are automatically destined to be leaders in the church.
Paul made it very clear to Timothy that spiritual leadership in the church has
very specific parameters and standards. Furthermore, those standards extend
beyond the leader to include the leader's spouse and family.

The first-century church recognized two clergy positions: bishop and
deacon.

The term *bishop* has been translated in other passages of the New Testament as overseer, elder or presbyter, and pastor. This person in spiritual
leadership was to be above ethical criticism (translated here as "blameless"),
married to only one wife, self-controlled, serious about matters of faith,
moral, hospitable, and able to teach. He was *not* to be a heavy drinker,
subject to angry outbursts, quarrelsome, covetous, or greedy. He was to be a
man who exercised godly authority in his home and had good relationships
with his wife and children. He was to have exhibited tried-and-true spiritual
maturity and leadership and humbly serve others. He was to have a good
reputation among those outside the church.

Paul made an interesting observation about the role of bishop. He said: If a person desires to be a bishop, he desires a good thing. There is nothing wrong with aspiring to be a person in spiritual leadership. To have this aspiration means that a person desires to *be* a person of spiritual maturity and excellent character.

The word *deacon* means *servant*. Deacons primarily functioned to help meet needs in the church. It was vital, said Paul, that deacons be reverent, able to communicate clearly and consistently, refrain from excess wine, and be free of any motive related to greed. They must freely forgive others and refuse to harbor grudges or bitterness. Only with this character profile could a deacon serve all in the church fairly, honestly, and freely. Paul admonished that deacons be tested in service, suggesting an internship-style training period. Like bishops, deacons were to be the husband of one wife and to exercise godly authority in their own homes. Their wives, perceived to be co-laborers in a ministry of service, were to be reverent, self-controlled, faithful, and without a bent toward gossip or slander.

Paul exalted the role of deacon, stating that deacons had a tremendous opportunity for both influence within the church and a strong witness to the outside world. The job of deacon was not to be despised, nor was it to be considered a second-rate role.

Although the names and roles of leadership in the modern church may vary from those outlined for Timothy, leadership in the church still tends to be of two general types: first, leadership that deals primarily with the *eternal* spiritual matters of God's truth, especially prayer and the preaching and teaching of God's Word and, second, leadership that is focused primarily on *earthly* needs, especially areas of practical service and relational ministries. Both types of leadership are vital.

In countless churches around the world, trained laity also tend to gravitate to one of these two types of ministry. Sunday school teachers, prayer group leaders, and Bible study leaders, for example, tend to fall into the spiritual leadership category. Those who lead outreaches to shut-ins, take meals to the grieving, or minister to those in the hospital tend to fall into the practical need-meeting category.

We each are wise to understand our unique bent toward one general category of ministry—whether as clergy or laity—and to prepare ourselves fully to exhibit the best leadership possible. We also are wise to respect and support those who do not have our specific bent. Above all, we each should aspire to become *qualified* to be leaders even if we are never elected to or tapped for a leadership position. We each should feel challenged to pursue the highest standards of moral behavior and seek to have a sterling reputation for godliness. There is no true leadership apart from character excellence and the development of a servant's heart.

What do you aspire to when it comes to your role in the church?

Are you geared more toward spiritual leadership or practical need-meeting areas of service?

How are you preparing yourself for a potential leadership position?

A
Application for Today

From the time Joe accepted Jesus as his personal Savior at age fifteen, he had a strong desire to work in the church. His father, however, wanted Joe to be a dentist and join the family dental practice. So, in an effort to gain approval from his father, Joe became a health sciences major when he enrolled in college. Finally, after four years of misery and a Bachelor of Science degree, Joe shared with his father the call of God he believed was on his life. He applied to and was accepted for seminary studies. Overnight, Joe began to enjoy academic life! From Bible courses to Hebrew and Greek language classes, from church history to liturgy to missions courses, Joe felt he was finally home.

After seminary, Joe accepted a job as the pastor of a small, rural church. He was enthusiastic about the church and loved the people, but nothing seemed to work well. He struggled with discouragement and eventually began to take medications to help with depression. "What's wrong with me?" Joe asked a man who had been a pastor for forty years.

After listening at length to Joe's story and Joe's self-appraisal of his current work, the senior pastor wisely counseled Joe, "You are called of God, Joe, to work in His church, but not as a pastor. You are very well equipped to be a church administrator and the director of a church educational program—perhaps even a Bible institute. But pastoral counseling, visiting the sick and dying, comforting the grieving, and ministries related to encouragement are not your strength. You are a good preacher, but by your own admission, you become impatient with your flock and seem to struggle with having the empathy and compassion you believe you should have as the pastor of your people. I know a pastor of a large church who is a wonderful pastor and a terrible administrator. I'm going to talk to him about you."

Within three months Joe was working at that larger church as the church administrator and the head of the church's educational program and publishing enterprises. He had found the focus for his ministry calling at last!

Do you know your distinctive ministry gifts?

If not, do you know how to begin to discover those gifts?

Are you using your ministry gifts?

Often people are talked into fulfilling church obligations or attempting some task at which they are mildly successful rather than trusting God to lead them to what He gifted them to do with *maximum* effectiveness and success. Is this the case with you? How can you guard against the tendency to do what *others* want you to do when you know, in your heart of hearts, they are not what God has required, designed, or equipped you to do?

S
Supplementary Scriptures to Consider

Paul wrote this to Titus on church leadership:

> For this reason I left you in Crete, that you should set in order the things that are lacking, and appoint elders in every city as I commanded you—If a man is blameless, the husband of one wife, having faithful children not accused of dissipation or insubordination. For a bishop must be blameless, as a steward of God, not self-willed, not quick-tempered, not given to wine, not violent, not greedy for money, but hospitable, a lover of what is good, sober-minded, just, holy, self-controlled, holding fast the faithful word as he has been taught, that he may be able, by sound doctrine, both to exhort and convict those who contradict (Titus 1:5–9).

• Compare this list of qualifications for a church overseer (bishop) with the list that the apostle Paul gave to Timothy.

• What do you believe it means for a church leader to be a "steward of God"?

• What does it mean to you to be a "lover of what is good"?

• Whether you are filling a clergy or laity role, do you feel equipped "by sound doctrine, both to exhort and convict" those who openly disagree with or contradict you? How might you become equipped to do this? Why should a minister have this ability?

The apostle Paul also wrote this to Timothy on the subject of church leadership:

> Let the elders who rule well be counted worthy of double honor, especially those who labor in the word and doctrine. For the Scripture says, "You shall not muzzle an ox while it treads out the grain," and "The laborer is worthy of his wages." Do not receive an accusation against an elder except from two or three witnesses (1 Tim. 5:17–19).

• Why is it important to honor those who rule well? What do you do in your church setting to honor those who minister in your midst?

• What does it mean to refrain from receiving an accusation against an elder?

• Note that the apostle Paul used the word *witnesses* when it came to accusations of elders. What is the difference between criticism based on feelings or differences of opinion, and genuine accusations based upon a person's behavior? Why is it important to deal only with accusations brought by two or three witnesses?

I
Introspection and Implications

1. Do you believe you are a minister in your church? In what ways? What would you state as your ministry job description?

2. The apostle Paul did not give details about who it is that evaluates a person for assignment as a bishop, deacon, or elder. Nor did the apostle Paul describe the process used for evaluation. How are candidates for leadership positions evaluated and selected in your church or denomination?

3. Have you ever encountered a person who eagerly aspired to be in ministry but who didn't seem remotely qualified to be a minister? What happened? Why do you believe such a person aspired to ministry in the first place?

4. Do you aspire to be a church leader? Why or why not?

C
Communicating the Good News

In what practical ways do you believe an evangelistic *messenger* of the gospel should display a good testimony among people in the world at large?

LESSON #4

WOMEN IN THE EARLY CHURCH

Chaste: behaving in a pure way

B
Bible Focus

> *I desire therefore that . . . the women adorn themselves in*
> *modest apparel, with propriety and moderation, not with*
> *braided hair or gold or pearls or costly clothing, but, which is*
> *proper for women professing godliness, with good works. Let*
> *a woman learn in silence with all submission. And I do not*
> *permit a woman to teach or to have authority over a man, but*
> *to be in silence (1 Tim. 2:8-12).*

Few sentences in the entire New Testament have evoked as much controversy in the modern church as those in this passage from Paul's letter to Timothy. To truly understand Paul's message we need to understand the greater audience to whom Paul was writing and understand the specific ways in which that culture is like our world today.

As a port city in what is modern-day Turkey, the city of Ephesus was at the end of the ancient silk and spice trade routes. Life in Ephesus was rich, colorful, cosmopolitan, and exotic. Ephesus freely imported merchandise from China and India, as well as from Egypt, Rome, northern Africa, and the port cities of Greece. Ephesus had a massive slave market, one of the largest amphitheaters in the ancient world, a major sporting complex, an opulent pagan temple, and a four-story library with an elaborate marble façade. The main streets of the city were marble, and many homes featured courtyards that housed small animals and birds from far-away places with strange-sounding names.

Like today's western world, the women of Ephesus were highly fashion conscious. Some of the women in the church came from pagan lifestyles. They probably dressed in the exotic, sensual styles associated with the pagan worship at the temple built for the Greek goddess Artemis (known as Diana to the Romans). As in many parts of the world today, the Ephesian women's jewelry and adornment often served as a billboard for the wealth and status of their husbands. Paul admonished the women in the church: do not use your clothing, hairstyles, or jewelry to draw attention to yourself, but rather adorn yourself and behave in a way that draws attention to Christ Jesus. Do not use fashion to gain status or a reputation for wealth and prosperity. These uses for fashion create division in the church. Rather, seek to develop character that reflects a genuine richness of spirit. Such behavior unites the church. Do not rely on outward appearance for your reputation, but rather live and work in a way that brings you recognition for spiritual excellence.

Paul was not trying to limit women as much as he was seeking to redirect their focus away from temporal outer trappings and toward lasting, eternal, and noble inner qualities.

When it came to spiritual education, Paul was *for* women! The typical pattern in Judaism was for men to sit at the front of a synagogue, where they engaged in prayer and in reading and discussing the law. Women sat behind the men—usually in an area separated by a latticework barrier or in something akin to a modern balcony. Gathered in their own section, somewhat removed from the action of the service, women tended to openly talk to their friends and other family members when they were at the synagogue. They generally paid little or no attention to the proceedings of the service. Paul said to them, in essence, "Stop talking among yourselves and listen intently to what is being read and said. Enter into the prayers. Learn the Scriptures. Hear what the preacher is preaching and the teacher is teaching." Paul wanted the women to be educated in spiritual matters and to know God's Word.

Finally, a woman in New Testament times was considered to be under her husband's protection and authority if she was married, or under her father's protection and authority if she was single. (If a woman was single and her father was deceased, she was under the protection and authority of her eldest brother or other designated male family member.) A woman who assumed administrative authority over a man or taught with authority over a man was setting up her husband or father to be over the person she was teaching or supervising. There simply was no provision in the greater cultures of Greece, Rome, or Judaism for this to occur. No woman had had the social ability to position one man over another man, directly or indirectly.

Furthermore, few women in the first-century church had the ability to read, and those who could did not have a background of studying or discussing the Scriptures. From early childhood, Jewish boys engaged in Torah study with older men; little girls were excluded from such study. Thus, Jewish female believers had a significant amount of catching up to do when it came to learning and discussing the law. Female Greek believers had no precedent *at all* for studying Scripture. They were starting at ground zero. Paul did not prohibit women from learning or studying. Rather, he encouraged it. His approach: learn as much as you can from those who currently know more! Stop talking and start studying diligently so you can catch up quickly!

Elsewhere in his letters, Paul encouraged women to teach other women, and he admonished older women to be role models for younger women. Paul did not exclude women from leadership; he sought to establish a way for women to grow into a full Scriptural understanding and exercise their leadership abilities while maintaining harmony within this new church.

How does this relate to women in the church today? All women should be encouraged to learn all they can about God's Word and teach in settings created to mutually edify the whole church. Every church and every denomination will determine for itself exactly who is qualified to teach and who should be that teacher's pupils. The challenge to women is the same challenge given to men: study God's Word!

Ask yourself today:

Do I dress and present myself to the world in ways that draw attention to Jesus Christ?

Do I value the development of inner qualities more than I value a display of outer wealth?

Do I ever use possessions to gain status or to exert personal power?

Am I a diligent student of God's Word? Am I learning all I can from the best teachers available to me?

Am I preparing myself to teach what I know to those who can benefit from what I have learned?

A
Application for Today

"How can you go to that church?" a woman asked her friend. "You are such a gifted speaker and you know the Bible so well, yet you would never be allowed to preach from the pulpit in that church, or even in that denomination!"

The friend hesitated and in the silence, the woman added, "And besides, they are so old-fashioned in their appearance."

"Let me address the fashion matter first," the friend responded. "I find it incredibly freeing *not* to feel any pressure to have expensive jewelry or the trendiest clothes and shoes. I like timeless, conservative styles. But that's really what is involved here, isn't it? It is a matter of style! Some churches seem to go for one style, some another. I'm comfortable with the style of this church. Frankly, I wouldn't feel comfortable in either a high-fashion church or a church where shorts, tank tops, and flip-flops are regular Sunday-morning dress."

"All right," the woman conceded. "I can see your point, but what about the fact that they keep you from certain positions solely because you are a woman?"

"I am plenty busy!" the friend replied. "I don't focus on what I am *not* asked or allowed to do. I focus on what I *am* asked and allowed to do. I teach Sunday school to adults, and forty-five minutes of teaching every Sunday is far more speaking opportunity than ten minutes in the pulpit every few months. I teach children in the summer camp program. I visit the sick and take meals to people who are newly home from hospitalization. I help provide and arrange flowers for the altar. My husband and I regularly open our home to visiting speakers and missionaries. I have plenty of opportunity to influence leaders in our church and learn from them at the same time."

The woman then added. "I understand your concerns. A friend of mine at the church asked the pastor about opportunities for women. He and others in the church compiled a list of thirty-eight opportunities for ministry in the church that openly and eagerly welcome women to participate. Women have tremendous influence at our church. They are not in the top leadership position as pastor, but much of what they do is pastoral."

She then concluded, "Frankly, I'm too busy doing what I love to do in the church to worry about what I am *not* doing."

Are you using church rules as an excuse for not getting more involved?

Are you using your spiritual and natural gifts to the maximum of your energy and ability?

Are you focused on what *can* be done more than on what *can't* be done?

Are you equating influence with authority? If so, consider how having influence might differ from having final say. What are the benefits of having influence without ongoing responsibility for rule-keeping or rule-setting?

S
Supplementary Scriptures to Consider

The apostle Paul wrote very specifically about widows who were in the church. It was customary in the Jewish community to provide sustenance for widows—shelter, food, and basic clothing—and for the widows, in turn, to spend their time in service to the community, primarily through prayer. True widows were those who had no children or other relatives who could care for them.

> Honor widows who are really widows. But if any widow has children or grandchildren, let them first learn to show piety at home and to repay their parents; for this is good and acceptable before God. Now she who is really a widow, and left alone, trusts in God and continues in supplications and prayers night and day. But she who lives in pleasure is dead while she lives. And these things command, that they may be blameless. But if anyone does not provide for his own, and especially for those of his household, he has denied the faith and is worse than an unbeliever.
>
> Do not let a widow under sixty years old be taken into the number, and not unless she has been the wife of one man, well reported for good works: if she has brought up children, if she has lodged strangers, if she has washed the saints' feet, if she has relieved the afflicted, if she has diligently followed every good work.

But refuse the younger widows; for when they have begun to grow wanton against Christ, they desire to marry, having condemnation because they have cast off their first faith. And besides they learn to be idle, wandering about from house to house, and not only idle but also gossips and busybodies, saying things which they ought not. Therefore I desire that the younger widows marry, bear children, manage the house, give no opportunity to the adversary to speak reproachfully. For some have already turned aside after Satan. If any believing man or woman has widows, let them relieve them, and do not let the church be burdened, that it may relieve those who are really are widows (1 Tim. 5:3–16).

• Apparently some in the church at Ephesus were claiming to be widows when they truly were not—they perhaps had been divorced or abandoned by their husbands. Others appear to have chosen to rely upon the benevolence of the church rather than work or seek to be married. They had turned into idle busybodies and gossips. What do you perceive to be the wisdom of Paul's admonitions to Timothy?

• Have you or someone you loved ever been the victim of vicious gossip? What was the result?

• Why is it better for a family to support its widows rather than to rely upon the church as a whole to do so? What are the implications for the broader society when families abdicate their responsibility and entrust the welfare of their loved ones to the government of the general population?

• Have you ever encountered a person who appeared to be using the church for personal benefit? What was the result for the person and for the church as a whole?

The apostle Paul gave specific instructions for the teaching of young people in the church, both men and women. He provided both a character profile and a curriculum, of sorts, for older men and women to follow:

> But as for you, speak the things which are proper for sound doctrine: that the older men be sober, reverent, temperate, sound in faith, in love, in patience; the older women likewise, that they be reverent in behavior, not slanderers, not given to much wine, teachers of good things—that they admonish the young women to love their husbands, to love their children, to be discreet, chaste, homemakers, good, obedient to their own husbands, that the word of God may not be blasphemed (Titus 2:1–5).

• How do you respond to the high character standards that the apostle Paul established for teachers? What is the importance of teachers having impeccable character? What are the dangers of having teachers in the church who may know their subject matter extremely well but have major character flaws?

• How do you respond to the curriculum that the apostle Paul admonished the older women to teach the younger women?

• Define, in very practical ways, these phrases:

Love their husbands:

Love their children:

Discreet:

Chaste:

Homemakers:

Good:

Obedient:

In his letter to Titus, the apostle Paul also provided a profile for Titus to exemplify as a leader and teacher, as well as a one-point curriculum for teaching younger men:

> Exhort the young men to be sober-minded, in all things showing yourself to be a pattern of good works; in doctrine showing integrity, reverence, incorruptibility, sound speech that cannot be condemned, that one who is an opponent may be ashamed, having nothing evil to say of you (Titus 2:6–8).

• What does it mean to you to be "sober-minded"? Why do you believe Paul emphasized this in the exhortation of young men?

• How do you respond to the character profile Paul gave to Titus? What does it mean to you for a person to display the following:

Show yourself to be a pattern of good works:

Show integrity in doctrine:

Show reverence:

Display incorruptibility:

Be a person of sound speech that cannot be condemned:

I
Introspection and Implications

1. Do you believe men and women tend to display authority in different ways? If so, how so? Do you believe men and women respond to authority in different ways? If so, how so? Do these responses differ according to the sex of the person in authority? In other words, do women respond differently to men in authority over them than to women in authority? Do men respond differently to men in authority over them than to women in authority?

2. Have you ever had a woman teacher you greatly admired and from whom you learned a great deal? What were her foremost character qualities? Are there any areas of life in which you would *not* have wanted her to be your teacher?

3. What do you perceive to be the best ways for any person to influence another person, regardless of the formal title or position the person might have?

C
Communicating the Good News

The apostle Paul gave no instructions about women functioning as evangelists or prophets. Indeed, there are women in the New Testament who were called prophetesses, and there were also women who appear to have had great influence in sharing the gospel with unbelievers and in teaching the basics of the gospel to new believers. Do you perceive gender differences as having a significant impact on evangelism?

LESSON #5

MARKS OF A
TRULY RICH LIFE

*Godliness: the character traits of God
manifested in human behavior*

B
Bible Focus

> *Now godliness with contentment is great gain. For we brought nothing into this world, and it is certain we can carry nothing out. And having food and clothing, with these we shall be content. But those who desire to be rich fall into temptation and a snare, and into many foolish and harmful lusts which drown men in destruction and perdition. For the love of money is a root of all kinds of evil, for which some have strayed from the faith in their greediness, and pierced themselves through with many sorrows. . . .*
>
> *Command those who are rich in this present age not to be haughty, nor to trust in uncertain riches but in the living God, who gives us richly all things to enjoy. Let them do good, that they be rich in good works, ready to give, willing to share, storing up for themselves a good foundation for the time to come, that they may lay hold on eternal life (1 Tim. 6:6–10, 17–19).*

Paul had nothing against money or wealth. He knew that money was a necessity for the basics of life and for accomplishing gospel-related goals. He also knew that striving for material wealth could sidetrack a person from pursuing eternal goals that will never find their way onto a financial statement. Paul wrote about eight wealth-related principles in his first letter to Timothy:

1. We bring nothing into this world and we can take nothing out of it when we die. All of life's getting and spending is an exercise in stewardship, which is allocating resources to their best possible use.

2. We should be content with having the basics of life. Paul cited food and clothing. Shelter could certainly be considered a basic of life.

3. Those who desire to be rich are subject to temptations related to the acquisition of money and material goods. A rich person's desire for more can easily turn to greed, and intense greed can readily result in crimes and sins, both of attitude and behavior. Note especially that Paul taught that the *love* of money can be a root of all kinds of evil, not money itself. What we love, we pursue. It is the pursuit of wealth that ensnares a person and keeps a person from pursuing true riches in Christ Jesus. A Christian's desire must be for the Lord and the accomplishment of His purposes, not a desire for material gain.

4. Those who have great wealth often become haughty, thinking themselves better than those who have less. The rich person must guard against this continually.

5. Those who have great wealth have a tendency to trust in their wealth rather than trust in God. Again, the rich person must be on guard against this.

6. The great challenge for the wealthy is to use their material resources to extend the gospel: producing good works, giving generously to those in need, and sharing liberally with fellow believers. This is what keeps the rich person's priorities right, produces eternal reward, and establishes a foundation that will enable a person or church group to transcend the difficulties of life.

7. Godliness with contentment is what we should seek to gain in this life—not material wealth.

Keep in mind that Paul was writing to Timothy, who was ministering to a large church in Ephesus, one of the most prosperous cities on earth during the first century. Ephesus was a great trading center, with overflowing abundance for some and slavery for others. The environment of Ephesus impacted the Christian church in ways that are very similar to what many believers face in today's global marketplace.

How do you personally respond to each of the principles Paul addressed? Do any of these statements especially challenge or convict you?

Do these principles resonate with your experience as a believer who may be living in a greedy, wealth-seeking environment?

How difficult is it for a Christian today not only to *believe* that "godliness with contentment is gain," but to live in a way that reduces life to basic needs with all excess going to extend the gospel?

A
Application for Today

"I don't think I'd fit in there," a woman said after her friend invited her to attend church together.

"Why not?" the friend asked.

"Well," the woman responded, "I don't have any difficulty relating to you—you work where I work, and you live in a neighborhood close to mine. But your church seems to have mostly people who aren't from our neighborhoods."

The woman who extended the invitation quickly perceived the root issue. The person she had invited was sending a message that she would feel uncomfortable worshiping alongside people from a lower socio-economic class. The poorer people in her church tended to belong to a different race.

"I felt the same way for a few weeks," the woman said, weighing her words carefully. "And then I got to know some of the people who are from other neighborhoods. I found that they loved God and their families, and when it came right down to our basic desire to follow Christ, we were the same. I learned a great deal about different cultures and what it is like to grow up in our nation without lots of material blessing. But I also discovered that through the months, the longer these new friends attended the church, the more they began to apply God's principles about money to their lives. They began to be more prosperous. I personally had a number of wonderful opportunities to help people discover new talents and find new opportunities for better jobs. It has been one of the most rewarding experiences of my life."

The woman who had been invited to attend the church nodded slightly but remained silent. Finally she said, "I'll think about that. I've been wanting to get involved in some kind of community service."

The friend who had extended the invitation replied cheerfully, "Great. I'll call you in a couple of weeks to see if you want me to pick you up on my way to church." As they went their separate ways, the woman said softly to herself, "Community service? I'm eager for you to fully embrace Christ Jesus! It might be just fine for you to come to my church to do a good work, but I'm going to believe that Christ Jesus is going to do a good work in *you* when you come, especially when it comes to your perspective on money and wealth."

Have you witnessed differences in socioeconomic status among the members of a church? How do you describe the dynamics of that type of congregation? Do you sense any bigotry or prejudice along financial lines?

Do you believe too much or too little time is spent preaching and teaching about financial matters in the church? Why so?

S
Supplementary Scriptures to Consider

In his second letter to Timothy, Paul warned that people in the last days will display a number of specific character and behavior traits:

> But know this, that in the last days perilous times will come: For men will be lovers of themselves, lovers of money, boasters, proud, blasphemers, disobedient to parents, unthankful, unholy, unloving, unforgiving, slanderers, without self-control, brutal, despisers of good, traitors, headstrong, haughty, lovers of pleasure rather than lovers of God, having a form of godliness but denying its power. And from such people turn away (2 Tim. 3:1–5)!

• What does it mean for a person to be a "lover of self"?

• What does it mean for a person to be a "lover of money"?

• Read through the list of behaviors that Paul gave to Timothy. Give examples of these behaviors and character traits that you see around you today:

    Boasters:

    Proud:

    Blasphemers:

Disobedience to parents:

Unthankful:

Unholy:

Unloving:

Unforgiving:

Slanderers:

Without self-control:

Brutal:

Despisers of good:

Traitors:

Headstrong:

Haughty:

Lovers of pleasure (rather than lovers of God):

• What does it mean for a person to have "a form of godliness" but deny its power?

• So many people display the ungodly traits the apostle Paul identified as contributing to peril in the last days. How does a person flee from all these people without becoming an isolationist?

In writing to Titus, the apostle Paul identified good works as one of the foremost purposes of money:

> Let our people also learn to maintain good works, to meet urgent needs, that they may not be unfruitful (Titus 3:14).

• How do you define or describe an *urgent* need?

• What are the challenges a person encounters in *maintaining* good works, as opposed to founding or establishing good works?

In writing to Titus, the apostle Paul said this about those who profess to know God but deny God in works:

> To the pure all things are pure, but to those who are defiled and unbelieving nothing is pure; but even their mind and conscience are defiled. They profess to know God, but in works they deny Him, being abominable, disobedient, and disqualified for every good work (Titus 1:15–16).

• What is the relationship between financial stewardship and the doing of good works?

• What is the link between engaging in doing works that match up to one's professions about God and becoming qualified for every good work?

Jesus taught:

> "No one can serve two masters; for either he will hate the one and love the other, or else he will be loyal to the one and despise the other. You cannot serve God and mammon" (Matt. 6:24).

• Have you ever struggled between serving the world's financial system and serving God? If so, how did you resolve that struggle?

I
Introspection and Implications

1. Have your opinions about money and wealth changed since you became a Christian? If so, how so?

2. What are the foremost lessons about money you have learned from a preacher, teacher, or fellow Christian at your church?

3. How do you guard against greed in your personal life?

4. Do you believe the rich are more uncomfortable around poor people or the poor are more uncomfortable around rich people? Why?

5. Do you believe the apostle Paul would approve completely with the way you handle money? Why or why not?

C
Communicating the Good News

What do you believe to be the relationship between finances and evangelism? Consider especially questions such as these:

- Do you believe that evangelistic and missionary efforts are properly funded in your church? If not, what might be done to encourage greater funding?

• Do you believe that a saving relationship with Christ Jesus automatically results in financial gain or loss?

• Is the gospel message financially neutral?

• Is there one gospel message that works better for prosperous nations or communities, and one that works better for poorer nations or communities?

If so, why so? If not, why not?

Lesson #6

THE PURSUIT OF RIGHTEOUSNESS

Stir up: kindle, to make something glow or to become bright

B
Bible Focus

> *But you, O man of God, flee these things and pursue righteousness, godliness, faith, love, patience, gentleness. Fight the good fight of faith, lay hold on eternal life, to which you were also called and have confessed the good confession in the presence of many witnesses (1 Tim. 6:11–12).*
>
> *I remind you to stir up the gift of God which is in you through the laying on of my hands. For God has not given us a spirit of fear, but of power and of love and of a sound mind.*
>
> *Therefore do not be ashamed of the testimony of our Lord, nor of me His prisoner, but share with me in the sufferings for the gospel according to the power of God, who has saved us and called us with a holy calling, not according to our works, but according to His own purpose and grace which was given to us in Christ Jesus before time began, but has now been revealed by the appearing of our Savior Jesus Christ, who has abolished death and brought life and immortality to light through the gospel, to which I was appointed a preacher, an apostle, and a teacher of the Gentiles. For this reason I also suffer these things; nevertheless I am not ashamed, for I know whom I have believed and am persuaded that He is able to keep what I have committed to Him until that Day.*
>
> *Hold fast the pattern of sound words which you have heard from me, in faith and love which are in Christ Jesus. That good thing which was committed to you, keep by the Holy Spirit who dells in us (2 Tim. 1:6–14).*

Paul admonished Timothy to *flee* from false teachers and from those who exhibited a love of money and were entering into "many foolish and harmful lusts" (1 Tim. 6:9) and instead, pursue righteousness—a life in right standing with God that bears the hallmarks of godliness, faith, love, patience, and gentleness. As part of a pursuit of righteousness, the apostle Paul advised Timothy to do three things.

First, Paul told Timothy to stir up the gift of God that had come to him through the laying on of Paul's hands, a gift generally identified as the anointing power of the Holy Spirit to preach and teach the gospel effectively. It was the Holy Spirit, Paul said, who would impart to Timothy power, love, and a sound mind, and remove from Timothy any spirit of fear.

How does one stir up the presence of God in his or her life? Perhaps the foremost way is to remain in constant daily communication with the Lord, inviting the Holy Spirit to do His work in us and through us, asking the Holy Spirit to reveal new insights into God's plans and purposes as we read the Bible, and to consult the Holy Spirit as we face every major choice and decision. Ongoing communication with the Holy Spirit keeps the Holy Spirit's working in us *alive and active!*

Second, Paul admonished Timothy to refrain from having any shame or embarrassment associated with either the gospel message or with Paul's sufferings. Paul did not want Timothy to regard any of his trials and tribulations as negating the power of the gospel, but to regard suffering as a badge of honor Paul wore gladly as Christ's preacher, apostle, and teacher of the Gentiles.

If a fellow believer is hit with a difficult set of circumstances, we must never allow ourselves to conclude that the difficulties are a result of weak faith. Nor should we conclude that their example for Christ has been tarnished irreversibly or that the gospel is ineffective. To the contrary! The way a person faces difficulties may very well provide a clear indication that the person's faith is strong, their trust in Christ is genuine, and the gospel enables them to endure and overcome life's struggles.

Third, Paul told Timothy to hold fast to the teachings Paul had imparted to him. Paul trusted Timothy to guard the accuracy and integrity of the gospel message and to teach other disciples as Paul had once taught Timothy.

It is the responsibility of every Christian to receive "the faith once delivered"—as the early church fathers wrote—and to pass it along without alteration. We are wise to memorize the Scriptures accurately, to teach our children to memorize the Scriptures, and to study the Scriptures thoroughly so that we see all commandments and principles in the context of the entire Word of God.

Paul wrote to Timothy as a fellow minister of the gospel, but even more so, as a fellow believer in and follower of Christ Jesus. His words to Timothy are words that apply to us all!

Is the Holy Spirit on active duty in your life today? If not, what might you do to stir up the Spirit's work in you?

Are there any aspects of your faith or the faith exhibited by a loved one, that give you cause for embarrassment? Why?

Do you believe you are being sufficiently diligent in passing on an accurate gospel message to others?

A
Application for Today

A man who had just experienced a major medical procedure found himself in an isolation unit of a hospital, and during three consecutive nights, he awoke suddenly in a panic, with intense fear and anxiety. He told his visiting pastor that, by day, he didn't seem to have fear. He had accepted Jesus as his personal Savior and believed he had a good relationship with God. He didn't have any particular fear of dying.

"Do you have a sense as to why you are afraid?" his pastor asked.

"I've been thinking about that," he said. "I've decided that I'm afraid of becoming an invalid and being totally dependent upon other people to care for me. I've always been very independent. I don't want to be a burden to others."

"You may need the help of others," his pastor said, "but perhaps only temporarily. Let me read a verse of the Bible to you." The pastor then read 2 Timothy 1:7. "God has not given us a spirit of fear, but of power and of love and of a sound mind."

The pastor went on to say, "The intense fear you are feeling is rooted in a lie that the devil is planting in your mind at the weakest part of your day. He very likely is telling you that you have no power over him or the circumstances of your life. He perhaps is lying to you that those who might be called upon to help care for you won't love you enough to help you fully. He perhaps is lying to you about your ability to believe that God loves you. The devil is also probably lying to you about your ability to balance your ideas related to dependence and independence."

The man nodded at each statement his pastor made. Tears welled up in his eyes. "You are right," he said. "Those are the thoughts I've been thinking when I awaken in the middle of the night."

"Here's what I want you to do," the pastor said. "When you awaken in fear, I want you to say aloud, 'Jesus, I trust You and put my faith fully in You. I thank You for giving my body the power to heal and for giving my spirit the power to believe. I thank You for loving me always and for assuring me that You are going to care for me and never forsake me. I thank You for giving me a sound mind to make wise decisions for my life. Thank You for healing me in body, mind, emotions, and spirit. I ask You to rebuke this spirit of fear and to give me a good night's sleep."

The pastor wrote out these statements on the white board at the foot of the man's bed, in bold letters. He then prayed with the man, asking him to recite each line as a prayer. As they said "Amen," the man said, "If I awaken tonight, I know just what to do."

The next day the pastor returned to find the man noticeably calmer and more cheerful. "It worked!" he said as soon as he saw his pastor walk into the room. "I barely made it through my prayer before I felt engulfed with peace and went back to sleep."

"Tonight," the pastor said, "I want you to pray this prayer *before* you prepare to sleep."

Are you ever overcome by intense fear or anxiety? What is your response? Have you isolated the exact nature of your fears?

How might the apostle Paul's words to Timothy help you? In what ways might you adapt the prayer this pastor wrote out to address your specific fears?

S
Supplementary Scriptures to Consider

In his second letter to Timothy, the apostle Paul urged Timothy to teach fully all that Paul had taught him, be willing to endure persecution, and remain steadfast in godly behavior, just as Paul had endured persecution and remained steadfast. He also held out to Timothy the privilege of being rewarded, just as Paul had been rewarded.

> You therefore, my son, be strong in the grace that is in Christ Jesus. And the things that you have heard from me among many witnesses, commit these to faithful men who will be able to teach others also. You therefore must endure hardship as a good soldier in Jesus Christ. No one engaged in warfare entangles himself with the affairs of this life, that he may please him who enlisted him as a soldier. And also if anyone competes in athletics, he is not crowned unless he competes according to the rules. The hardworking farmer must be first to partake of the crops. Consider what I say, and may the Lord give you understanding in all things (2 Tim. 2:1–7).

• In what ways are you purposefully and intentionally seeking to share what you know about the Lord with your children, grandchildren, or other members of your family? Are you actively involved in sharing with new believers what you have learned through the years about being a faithful Christian? If not, how might you begin to share more openly?

• What does it mean to you for a person to be "entangled" with the "affairs of this life"? How does a person keep from being entangled?

• Why is it important for a person to feel a sense of practical, tangible reward? What is the relationship between reward and an ability to withstand hardship?

The apostle Paul had taught Timothy well, including teaching him to *how* to teach. Paul also admonished Timothy in his second letter to *continue* to learn and teach:

> Be diligent to present yourself approved to God, a worker who does not need to be ashamed, rightly dividing the word of truth. But shun profane and idle babblings, for they will increase to more ungodliness (2 Tim. 2:15–16).

• What does it mean to you to "rightly divide" the word of truth? What is produced for the benefit of the believer who does this?

• Can you cite examples of "profane and idle babblings" in your world today? Have you witnessed ways in which they produce ungodliness?

The apostle Paul gave this detailed definition of an honorable life that is sanctified and useful to God:

> But in a great house there are not only vessels of gold and silver, but also of wood and clay, some for honor and some for dishonor. Therefore if anyone cleanses himself from the latter, he will be a vessel for honor, sanctified and useful for the Master, prepared for every good work. Flee also youthful lusts; but pursue righteousness, faith, love, and peace with those who call on the Lord out of a pure heart. But avoid foolish and ignorant disputes, knowing that they generate strife. And a servant of the Lord must not quarrel but be gentle to all, able to teach, patient, in humility correcting those who are in opposition, if God perhaps will grant them repentance, so that they may know the truth, and that they may come to their senses and escape the snare of the devil, having been taken captive by him to do his will (2 Tim. 2:20–26).

• Read the above passage once more, aloud and slowly. Is there a particular word, phrase, or sentence that you find challenging or convicting? How do you believe the Holy Spirit may be guiding you to make a change in your life?

The apostle Paul's wisdom to Timothy applies to all believers:

> I charge you therefore before God and the Lord Jesus Christ, who will judge the living and the dead at His appearing and His kingdom: Preach the word! Be ready in season and out of season. Convince, rebuke, exhort, with all longsuffering and teaching. For the time will come when they will not endure sound doctrine, but according to their own desires, because they have itching ears, they will heap up for themselves teachers; and they will turn their ears away from the truth, and be turned aside to fables. But you be watchful in all things, endure afflictions, do the work of an evangelist, fulfill your ministry (2 Tim. 4:1–5).

• What does it mean to "be ready in season and out of season"? How do you keep yourself ready to share the gospel at all times?

• Paul spoke of people having "itching ears" that caused them to turn from those who taught truth to those who taught fables. What does this mean to you today?

The apostle Paul encouraged Titus to deal with those under his leadership "with all authority":

> Speak these things, exhort, and rebuke with all authority. Let no one despise you (Titus 2:15).

• How do we speak "with all authority"? Is this learned? Is it a gift from the Holy Spirit?

• How might a strong leader stand up in a godly way to those who appear to despise them and what they teach?

The apostle Paul wrote to Timothy that there is a mystery associated with godliness:

> I write so that you may know how you ought to conduct
> yourself in the house of God, which is the church of the living
> God, the pillar and ground of the truth. And without contro-
> versy great is the mystery of godliness:
>> God was manifested in the flesh,
>> Justified in the Spirit,
>> Seen by angels,
>> Preached among the Gentiles,
>> Believed on in the world,
>> Received up in glory (1 Tim. 3:15–16).

• What aspects of godliness are a mystery to you?

• How does the example of Jesus inspire you to pursue a godly life?

I
Introspection and Implications

1. What is the most challenging aspect of being righteous? How do you respond to that challenge in your personal life?

2. The apostle Paul taught that all believers have responsibilities to exert leadership and influence for the gospel. What is the most challenging aspect of leadership you face? How do you respond to that challenge?

3. A man once said, "Accepting Jesus as Savior is easy. Following Jesus as Lord is the most difficult thing a person will ever do." Respond to that statement. In what specific ways do you agree or disagree?

4. How do you respond to the word godliness? Does it seem to be an unattainable goal? Is it a mystery? What do you believe the Holy Spirit may be challenging you to do?

C
Communicating the Good News

Some unbelievers say the church sets too high a standard when it comes to character and behavior; some even claim it is an impossible standard. How would you respond?

In what ways does the Holy Spirit *enable* us to lead a godly life? What role should the enabling power of the Holy Spirit have in our evangelistic messages about Jesus as Savior?

LESSON #7

THE MERCY OF GOD

*Mercy: kindness or forgiveness shown
to an offender or somebody a person
has power over*

B
Bible Focus

> *I thank Christ Jesus our Lord who has enabled me, because He counted me faithful, putting me into the ministry, although I was formerly a blasphemer, a persecutor, and an insolent man; but I obtained mercy because I did it ignorantly in unbelief. And the grace of our Lord was exceedingly abundant, with faith and love which are in Christ Jesus. This is a faithful saying and worthy of all acceptance, that Christ Jesus came into the world to save sinners, of whom I am chief. However, for this reason I obtained mercy, that in me first Jesus Christ might show all longsuffering, as a pattern to those who are going to believe on Him for everlasting life. Now to the King eternal, immortal, invisible, to God who alone is wise, be honor and glory forever and ever. Amen. (1 Tim. 1:12–17).*

Paul never lost sight of the truth that he was the recipient of God's great mercy. Throughout his post-conversion years, regardless of how spiritually mature he became, Paul remained intensely thankful for his salvation. He knew without doubt that he had been an unworthy sinner who had not received the justice he was due, but had received an outpouring of grace almost too glorious to grasp. Paul was exceedingly thankful to the Lord on two main accounts.

First, Paul was thankful that God had chosen him to be a recipient of His exceedingly abundant grace. Paul had done nothing to earn or deserve Christ. He had not sought out Christ to love Him. Rather, Christ, in His love, had sought out Paul.

This is not only true for Paul, but for each of us. We did not pursue a relationship with God. As the prophet Isaiah said with great accuracy: "All we like sheep have gone astray; we have turned, every one, to his own way" (Isaiah 53:6). In truth, God pursued a relationship with us—He found us, rescued us, and brought us into His fold.

Are you genuinely thankful for your salvation today?

Do you recognize fully that you did nothing to warrant the mercy of God; your salvation is pure gift?

A continually-kindled attitude of gratitude for what Jesus did on our behalf not only keeps us from becoming proud, but it helps us have faith that God can and will extend His mercy to our loved ones who have not yet received God's free gift of salvation.

Second, Paul was thankful that God had put him into the ministry. Paul knew who he had been and knew that *what* he had done had not qualified him from the honor of proclaiming the gospel as an evangelist, establishing churches as an apostle, and serving the Lord as a teacher and disciple-maker. Paul had been a blasphemer of Christ, a persecutor of Christians, and an insolent man filled with pride and self-righteousness. Even so, God had chosen Paul for ministry so that the change in his life might inspire others to believe this truth: *nobody* is beyond God's redemptive, transformative power.

God has called each Christian to some form of ministry, which in its basic form is helping another person to know Christ and follow Him closely. What a privilege we each have to bear the name of Christ and to extend His love to those who are desperately in need of His forgiveness and empowerment! Ministry is a calling, not a job. It is a privilege, not a chore.

Are you thankful today for the ministry to which God has called you and in which He is using you?

Are you trusting Him to lead, guide, and empower you so that all you do might bring lasting glory to His name?

A
Application for Today

"What are you praying for *yourself*?" a pastoral counselor asked a young man.

"Oh, I don't ask God for anything for *myself*," the young man said. "I ask God to help my mother, who is a widow, and to help my friends who are sick or have problems. But I would never ask God to do something for *me*."

"Why not?" the counselor asked.

"Well, that would be selfish," he said.

"Even if what you asked was clearly in keeping with a godly life?"

The young man thought for a moment and then said, "It would still seem self-centered, I think. I've been taught all my life that God wants people to be humble, not proud."

Having already established the fact that the young man had accepted Jesus as his Savior, the counselor asked, "Do you believe God saved you because you were humble?"

"I don't know," the young man said.

"Think about that question," the counselor suggested. "And let me give you several more questions to consider:

"First, is thinking of yourself as unworthy of God's mercy and salvation the same thing as humility?

"Second, now that you have accepted God's mercy and forgiveness, are you still unworthy?

"Third, as part of your salvation and ongoing faithful walk in Christ Jesus, does God regard you as worthy or unworthy of a ministry role in the church?

"Fourth, does a person need God's blessings to be the most effective minister possible?"

"And finally, if the New Testament teaches that we lack some things because we do not ask God for them, what is wrong with asking God for His blessings that will further equip us for effective ministry" (James 4:2)?

How would *you* answer each of the questions posed by this counselor?

S
Supplementary Scriptures to Consider

The apostle Paul wrote to Titus about the life that is transformed by Christ:

> The grace of God that brings salvation has appeared to all men, teaching us that, denying ungodliness and worldly lusts, we should live soberly, righteously, and godly in the present age, looking for the blessed hope and glorious appearing of our great God and Savior Jesus Christ, who gave Himself for us, that He might redeem us from every lawless deed and purify for Himself His own special people, zealous for good works (Titus 2:11–14).

• In this passage what did Paul identify as the great lessons we are to learn from the grace of God?

• Do you have a keen sense that you have been purified and are part of a "special people" of God? If not, why not? If so, how so?

- In what ways do you believe you have been "redeemed from every lawless deed"?

- Are you zealous for good works? If not, what might be necessary for you to become zealous for good works?

The apostle Paul also wrote to Titus about God's mercy:

> For we ourselves were also once foolish, disobedient, deceived, serving various lusts and pleasures, living in malice and envy, hateful and hating one another. But when the kindness and the love of God our Savior toward man appeared, not by works of righteousness which we have done, but according to His mercy He saved us, through the washing of regeneration and renewing of the Holy Spirit, whom He poured out on us abundantly through Jesus Christ our Savior, that having been justified by His grace we should become heirs according to the hope of eternal life (Titus 3:3–7).

- Respond to this statement: "We are incapable of transforming our own sinful *nature*."

- Many people—both in the church and in the world—believe it is possible for a person to earn God's kindness, love, and eternal life by their own works of righteousness (good works). How do you personally address those who hold such a belief?

I
Introspection and Implications

1. What is the difference between considering yourself unworthy of God's blessings as a "natural man" and seeing yourself as qualified for all of God's blessings in Christ Jesus because you are a Christian and a spiritually-regenerated?

2. Are you as thankful today for your salvation as you were on the day you received Jesus as your Savior? When was the last time you thanked the Lord for your salvation? When was the last time you gave a public word of testimony about your salvation? What about the next time?

3. Under each of the headings below, list several words that describe your life before you became a Christian and after you accepted Jesus as your Savior:

                Before Christ   **After Christ**

4. In what ways do you perceive God has used or is using your before-and-after example to teach or encourage others?

C
Communicating the Good News

Many people today regard themselves as *good* people and, as such, do not see themselves as needing a Savior. How do we effectively share the gospel with them?

How might we more effectively explain or illustrate the mercy of God in our evangelistic messages?

Reread Titus 3:3–7 above. How might we best convey the "kindness and love of God" to unbelievers?

NOTES TO LEADERS
OF SMALL GROUPS

As the leader of a small discussion group, think of yourself as a facilitator with three main roles:

- Get the discussion started.

- Involve every person in the group.

- Encourage an open, candid discussion that remains Bible-focused.

You certainly don't need to be the person with all the answers! In truth, much of your role is to be a person who asks questions:

- What really impacted you most in this lesson?

- Was there a particular part of the lesson or a question that you found troubling?

- Was there a particular part of the lesson that you found encouraging or insightful?

- Was there a particular part of the lesson that you'd like to explore further?

Express to the group at the outset of your study that your goal as a group is to gain new insights into God's Word; this is not the forum for defending a point of doctrine or a theological opinion. Stay focused on what God's Word says and means. The purpose of the study is also to share insights on how to apply God's Word to everyday life. *Every* person in the group can and should contribute. The collective wisdom that flows from Bible-focused discussion is often very rich and deep.

Seek to create an environment in which every member of the group feels free to ask questions of other members in order to gain greater understanding. Encourage the group members to voice their appreciation to one another for new insights gained and be supportive of one another. Take the lead in this. Genuinely appreciate and value the contributions made by each person.

Since the letters of Paul are geared to our personal Christian lives as well as to the life of the church as a whole, you may experience a tendency in your group sessions to become overly critical of your *own* church or church leaders. Avoid the tendency to create discord or dissatisfaction. Don't use this Bible study as an opportunity to spread rumor, air anyone's dirty laundry, or criticize your pastor. Rather, seek positive ways to build up one another, including your church leaders. Seek positive outcomes and solutions to any problems you may identify.

You may want to begin each study by having one or more members of the group read through the section provided under "Bible Focus." Ask the group specifically if it desires to discuss any of the questions under the "Application" section, the "Supplemental Scriptures" section, and the "Implications" and "Communicating the Gospel" sections. You do not need to bring closure—or come to a definitive conclusion or consensus—about any one question asked in this study. Rather, if the group does not *have* a satisfactory Bible-based answer , encourage them to engage in further "asking, seeking, and knocking" strategies to discover the answers! Remember the words of Jesus: "Ask, and it will be given to you, seek, and you will find; knock, and it will be opened to you. For everyone who asks receives, and he who seeks finds, and to him who knocks it will be opened" (Matthew 7:7–8).

Finally, open and close your study with prayer. Ask the Holy Spirit, whom Jesus called the Spirit of Truth, to guide your discussion and to reveal what is of eternal benefit to you individually and as a group. As you close your study, ask the Holy Spirit to seal to your remembrance what you have read and studied and to show you in the upcoming days, weeks, and months *ways* to apply what you have studied to your daily life and relationships.

General Themes for the Lessons

Each lesson in this study has one or more core themes. Continually pull the group back to these themes. You can do this by asking simple questions, such as, "How does that relate to _____?" or "How does that help us better understand the concept of _____?" or "In what ways does that help us apply the principle of _____?"

A summary of general themes or concepts in each lesson is provided below:

Lesson #1

THE IMPORTANCE OF SOUND DOCTRINE

Living out the commandments of God vs. freedom in Christ Jesus

Finding a balance between negative don'ts and positive do's

Lesson #2

PRAYING FOR THOSE IN AUTHORITY

Praying for leaders in government

Praying for leaders in the church

Praying for leaders in your place of employment, service, or neighborhood

Lesson #3

QUALIFICATIONS FOR CHURCH LEADERSHIP

Spiritual leadership issues

Practical leadership issues

Having a servant's attitude as a leader

Lesson #4

WOMEN IN THE EARLY CHURCH

The value of chaste and modest behavior displayed by all believers

The submission required in all *learning*

Lesson #5

MARKS OF A TRULY RICH LIFE

The godly use of money

Overcoming temptations related to greed and the tendency to trust in riches

How to have "godliness with contentment" in a highly materialistic society

Lesson #6

THE PURSUIT OF RIGHTEOUSNESS

Stirring up the gifts of God

Overcoming a spirit of fear

Developing a pattern of sound words and godly behavior

Lesson #7

THE MERCY OF GOD

The abundant grace of God

The testimony of a transformed life

The redemptive work of Christ Jesus, which we cannot accomplish by our own will or goodworks